Charlie's
Beach Adventure
with Luna

This book belongs to:

✶✶

For Charlie.

To my beautiful Charlie 'bear', my faithful companion and cherished 'furry' friend. Together, we explored the world, creating memories and sharing adventures.

In your memory, this book celebrates the joy and love you brought into my life. You'll always hold a special place in my heart. This book is dedicated to you and all those who have lost their beloved four-legged friends.

Charlie woke up to a beautiful sunny day and she knew exactly what she wanted to do.

"I want to go to the beach today!" she said excitedly, wagging her tail.

As she got ready for her beach adventure, Charlie collected all the things she needed to take to the beach including her favourite pair of pink sunglasses.

Charlie quickly gathered everything she needed and headed out the door.

But as she was walking, Charlie realised that she didn't want to go to the beach alone.

"I wonder if Luna wants to come with me," she thought to herself.

Luna was one of Charlies best friends and they had lots of exciting adventures together.

Charlie made a quick stop at Luna's house and knocked on the door.

Luna was very excited to go to the beach with Charlie and quickly gathered all the things she needed.

Soon enough, the two best friends were on their way to the beach.

As they walked to the beach, Charlie and Luna could hear the seagulls squawking in the distance. They arrived and found a perfect spot to lay their towels.

They both ran into the sea and were having too much fun to notice how cold the water was. After they went for a doggy paddle, Luna showed Charlie how to jump over the waves and soon they were jumping over bigger and bigger waves.

After their swim, they shook off the water and sat down on their towels to eat their sandwiches. But, before Luna could take a bite, a big, white, noisy seagull swooped down and stole her sandwich.

"That's my sandwich!" shouted Luna at the seagull.

"Quick, let's see if we can get it back from him," said Charlie, running after the seagull.

But the seagull was too fast for Luna and Charlie, and he flew away with the sandwich hanging out of his beak.

"What a naughty seagull!" exclaimed Charlie.

Luna was upset about the seagull stealing her sandwich, but Charlie came to the rescue. She offered to share her peanut butter and cheese sandwiches with Luna.

Charlie could have easily eaten her own sandwich and left Luna hungry, but instead, she knew the right thing to do was to share her sandwiches.

This made Luna happy and it made Charlie feel good too.

They quickly ate Charlie's sandwich before the naughty seagull could come back for more.

After they had shared their lunch, Charlie suggested they build a sandcastle together.

They worked hard all afternoon and decorated their sandcastle with shells and interesting things they found on the beach.

It took them all afternoon to build their sandcastle. They were very tired when they had finished.

"I'm tired and sleepy now after all our hard work," Luna said. "Shall we go home?"

Charlie agreed and they packed up their things.

As they walked back home, Luna said, "Thank you for sharing your sandwich with me Charlie, your kindness meant a lot. I would have been very hungry if you hadn't shared your lunch with me".

Charlie smiled and she was pleased she had done the right thing.

Charlie smiled and wagged her tail. "You are welcome. I'm glad you had fun Luna. I had fun at the beach today too. It was perfect!"

As Charlie and Luna walked back home, Charlie realised that she had learned an important lesson that day. She had always known that sharing was important, but today she saw the true meaning of it.

From then on, Charlie and Luna made it a habit to share everything, not just with each other but also with their other friends. They learned that sharing brings everyone closer together and makes the world a happier place.

The End.

Puzzle & Colouring Fun
How many can you spot?

How many pairs of sunglasses can you spot in this book? _____

How many pink buckets can you spot in this book? _____

How many purple buckets can you spot in this book? _____

How many seagulls can you spot in this book? _____

Can you help Charlie get through the maze to Luna?

Can you colour in Charlie in her Garden?

Can you colour in Charlie & Luna's sandcastle?

Printed in Great Britain
by Amazon